796.62
TU

ultra sports

marathon cycling

by Chérie Turner

This book is dedicated to Keith McKee, who, among many other things, inspires me to keep riding my bike and writing books.

Published in 2002 by The Rosen Publishing Group, Inc.
29 East 21st Street, New York, NY 10010

Library of Congress Cataloging-in-Publication Data

Turner, Chérie.
Marathon cycling / by Chérie Turner.— 1st ed.
p. cm. — (Ultra sports)
Includes bibliographical references and index.
Summary: An exploration of marathon bicycling, including the history of the sport, profiles of famous riders, and beginners' tips on training, safety, gear, and types of events.
ISBN 0-8239-3553-1 (lib. bdg.)
1. Cycling—Juvenile literature. 2. Bicycle racing—Juvenile literature. [1. Bicycles and bicycling. 2. Bicycle racing.] I. Title. II. Series.
GV1043.5 .T87 2002
796.6'2—dc21

2001004765

Manufactured in the United States of America

contents

It's 2 AM, dark, windy, and cold. A lone racer rides her bicycle up a grueling twelve-mile climb. She's tired, and her feet ache. She hasn't slept for more than three hours in the last forty-two. Determined to keep going until the end, she focuses on keeping a positive attitude. She is not even halfway to the finish.

There are many different types of marathon or ultra distance cycling events. But whatever the form, ultra cycling pushes athletes to their physical and mental limits. Ultra distance cycling may be in the form of a race—like the Race Across America (RAAM), which features over 2,900 miles of nonstop riding—or simply an organized ride like a double century (200-mile) ride. You can cycle on

Ultra cycling forces people to test their limits in the toughest circumstances.

dirt or paved roads. Ultra cycling can be done with the help of others (supported) or alone (unsupported). An ultra event may last for less than one day or may take upward of a week or more. In some ultra events, cyclists ride for a certain amount of time—like in the increasingly popular twenty-four-hour mountain-bike races— while in others, they ride a certain distance.

In general, an ultra cycling event, like any ultra event, tests a person's mental and physical strength over a long period of time or a long distance. Rob Kish, who competes in many ultra races supported by a group of people, or crew, says that "ultra cycling is an extreme and intense individual effort complemented by focused team coordination of mental, physical, emotional, and environmental challenges . . . and problem solving over an extended period of time." Cyclist Chris Kostman sums up ultra cycling in an article called "Planet Ultra: It's Just an Attitude" published in *City Sports, Over the Edge,* and *UltraCycling*: "One word explains the difference between ultra athletes and the rest of the athletic masses: attitude." He goes on to say that those with the "attitude" see no limits. For the ultra athlete, nothing is impossible.

In this book, you will learn how to get started in the sport of ultra cycling, how people stay safe and healthy when participating in this demanding sport, what equipment is needed, what the cyclists who have been there have to say, and, finally, about different ultra cycling events. The world of ultra distance cycling is challenging, rewarding, and open to anyone with the will, and the attitude, to complete the ride. After reading this book, you may be inspired to get on a bike and start training for that first event. After that, who knows how far you'll go?

The History of Long-Distance Cycling

Ultra cycling unofficially started in 1891 in France. In that year, the first long-distance cycling race was held: the 600-kilometer (384-mile) Bordeaux-Paris (it ran from the city of Bordeaux to the city of Paris). This event inspired newspaper publisher and avid cyclist Pierre Griffard to organize the first running of the now-famous 1200-kilometer (756-mile) Paris-Brest-Paris (also called the PBP, the race runs from Paris to Brest and then back to Paris). In 1901, Griffard's publishing rival Henri Desgranges took control of the PBP. Desgranges also started the Tour de France in 1903—one of the world's most popular and challenging sporting events today. In 1904, Desgranges formed the first long-distance cycling organization in Paris, France: Audax Club Parisien (ACP). *Audax* is French for "to dare." The club promoted long-distance riding for "cycling enthusiasts." According to cycling organization

Randonneuring USA (RUSA), "The [ACP] standard was to ride 200 kilometers [120 miles] between dusk and dawn, always as a group." Some of these group rides even dared to cover distances as far as 300 and 400 kilometers (186 and 248 miles, respectively).

Things changed dramatically in 1921 when—according to ultra cycling historian Bill Bryant—"the 'always riding in a group' Audax format was abandoned by the Audax Club Parisien, and the self-paced 'allure libre' format was adopted." That is, riders were allowed to ride at their own pace and not remain within a group. Many riders preferred not being confined to a group. The ACP then created what soon became standard self-paced distances: 200, 300, 400, 600, 1,000, and 1,200 kilometers (124, 186, 248, 372, 621, and 750 miles, respectively).

But not everyone was pleased with this change in riding format. In fact, Desgranges was so upset that he created a rival club, Union des Audax Parisien, which continued to promote group riding. There was a great feud between the two clubs, each trying to prove that its style of riding produced better cyclists. Eventually, the self-paced format became the preference for most riders. The ACP remains the organization that oversees these self-paced rides, which are now held all over the world.

Randonneuring

The style of riding started by the ACP became known as randonneuring. To randonneur means to "go on a long trip, tour, outing, or ramble, usually on foot or on a bicycle," according to the RUSA Web site. Randonneuring events became known as brevets

Cyclists racing in the Tour de France, one of the oldest ultra sports events, in 1951

(which roughly means certificate). The standard brevet distances are the same as those established by the ACP over eighty years ago. Also, the ACP requires that each ride be completed within a certain amount of time (13.5 hours for 200 km, 20 hours for 300 km, 27 hours for 400 km, 40 hours for 600 km, and 75 hours for 1,000 km). To make sure that a rider completes the distance within the time limit, he or she is given a brevet card at the beginning of a ride. The card is stamped and the time is noted by ride officials at checkpoints—places along the route where the rider must check in. The card then serves as a record for the rider to show that he has completed the brevet.

It is important to remember that brevets are not races. For this reason, professionally licensed bicycle racers are not allowed to participate in any randonneuring event until they have not held a racing license for at least two years.

When participating in a randonneuring event, a rider must be self-supported—he or she must have everything needed to complete the event. The rider is allowed assistance only at a checkpoint. He or she must carry all food (or the money to buy it), lights, clothing—anything necessary to finish the ride. The only services ride organizers provide are limited to timing the riders, providing course directions, and setting up checkpoints along the course.

After the ACP brevets became popular, the club organized the Brevets de Randonneurs Européen (Brevets of European Randonneurs) in 1976 and the Brevets de Randonneurs Mondiaux (Brevets of Worldwide Randonneurs) in 1983. Each of these organizations makes sure that randonneuring clubs in Europe and all over the world adhere to ACP rules. These rules and traditions have been in place since those first rides over 100 years ago.

Randonneuring is the oldest form of organized ultra cycling, and it still exists today. Currently there are twenty-eight registered member organizations of Randonneurs Mondiaux, according to Jennifer Wise of RUSA. RUSA itself has a membership of over 1,100 riders.

Ultra Marathon Cycling

Another organization that has had a great impact on the long-distance cycling world is the Ultra Marathon Cycling Association (UMCA). Founded in 1980 by Lon Haldeman, John Marino, and Michael

Cycling clubs and organizations have grown and changed since the beginning of the twentieth century.

Shermer, the interests of the organization are simple: The UMCA is "dedicated to the advancement of long-distance bicycling." And it has done a terrific job, most notably in 1982, when the founders, along with cycling legend John Howard, created and promoted the world's most challenging nonstop bicycle race: the Great American Bike Race. This event started on the West Coast of the United States and finished on the East Coast—over 2,900 miles of racing! Renamed the Race Across America (RAAM) in 1983, it has run every year since. It remains one of the most demanding and difficult sporting events in the world. Because it seemed so extreme and unique in the early 1980s, ABC (American Broadcasting Company) television's *Wide World of*

Sports televised RAAM, bringing a lot of attention to this little-known sport. The UMCA has also promoted many other long-distance bicycle events, among them several twenty-four-hour and twelve-hour events.

Ultra Fever

As a result of the popularity of ultra sporting events in general, and the events promoted by organizations such as the UMCA, many other ultra cycling events have appeared on the scene. In particular, the ever growing interest in mountain biking has inspired the creation of numerous 100-mile and twenty-four-hour events.

The 24 Hours of Adrenalin series started in Canada in 1994, consisting of only one race and 170 racers. Today, the series promotes ten twenty-four-hour events held at locations throughout the United States and Canada. Over 9,000 racers and more than 27,000 spectators participate. In all, there are about thirty-five twenty-four-hour events across North America! There is also the Leadville 100, a 100-mile mountain-bike race in the Colorado Rocky Mountains.

For cyclists who prefer paved roads, road-bike events are held almost year-round throughout the United States and Canada. Riders have their pick of centuries (100-mile rides), double centuries (200-mile rides), numerous randonneuring rides, and more. For those looking for an even more extreme challenge, there is the prestigious Furnace Creek 508 (FC508), a 508-mile race through the California desert.

Today's Ultra Cycling

Interest in ultra cycling has grown tremendously in recent years. Even just thirty years ago, riding more than 100 miles was an event only the most extreme cyclists tackled. And mountain bikes didn't even exist!

Today, more and more people are taking an interest in riding long distances and racing through the night. And there are opportunities for every level of cyclist. Ultra cycling is no longer seen as the domain of the dedicated few. Riders can choose from a wide variety of distances. A rider can choose to go solo, completing the distance alone, or join a relay team and take turns with teammates. Whatever the interest level, there are events for anyone interested in long-distance cycling.

Fourteen-year-olds Stewart and KJ loved riding their bikes. They'd cycle to school and after school. On weekends, they'd map out routes and go exploring. This was the ultimate freedom and always a fantastic adventure. Over the months, their rides got longer and longer. Within a year, they were going as far as eighty miles in one day! Then, KJ learned about a ride that was going to happen in a nearby town. It was a double century: 200 miles! They decided to do it. Stewart and KJ talked to Oren, the local bike shop owner, and he helped them create a training program that

Having the help and support of training partners can enhance your preparation for an ultra cycling event.

would prepare them for the big ride. They were excited and made sure to train exactly as Oren suggested.

The ride was tough, but it was so exciting to travel all that way on a bike. They had endless stories for their friends and family. And they met many experienced riders who offered advice and information about training, equipment, riding technique, and local clubs. After relaxing and recovering for a couple of days, Stewart and KJ joined their local cycling club and started looking for their next challenge.

To get started as an ultra rider, all you really need is a bike, a helmet, and the will to ride. Certainly, as you advance, you will discover other equipment that you find helpful. To compete with the best, a rider needs years of training, proper nutrition, a lot of support, and even some luck. But that all comes in time.

Consider the story of ultra legend Lon Haldeman. While in junior high school, Haldeman enjoyed riding his one-speed bike. Back then, five miles was a long way for him to go. Over time, he started going for longer and longer rides. He enjoyed exploring and mapping out new adventures. Eventually, he and a friend completed a 100-mile ride. The next year, at age eighteen, he completed 200 miles. A year later, he went 300 miles, and in the following year, 400. Haldeman eventually went on to complete a double transcontinental ride (riding across the United States twice) in 1980. In 1982, he won the first RAAM (then called the Great American Bike Race). He continues to promote ultra cycling today as the codirector (with his wife and ultra legend Susan Notorangelo) of RAAM and co-owner, also with Notorangelo, of an ultra touring company called PAC Tours. But it all started with that one-speed bike and a map, and young Lon dressed in cut-off shorts and gym shoes.

Your First Challenge

To get started in the sport of ultra cycling, it is best to choose an event that is challenging but not overwhelming. For many people who want to get a taste of ultra cycling, a century (100-mile) ride is a good first event. Being a part of a relay team is another great way to test one's ultra abilities. Joining the support team or crew of a more experienced racer can also give you a feel for what is it like to participate in an ultra race. By crewing, you can learn about ultra racing and then apply that knowledge when you ride in an event.

Training

To get ready for an ultra event, you must train. Training involves preparing the body as well as the mind. In general, you want to slowly build endurance, strength, and confidence to the point where you feel that you can complete the challenge.

To train your body, you need to ride. To get the most out of your training, you should follow a program geared toward enabling you to complete your desired distance. In an article for *UltraCycling* magazine, ultra rider and bike racer Lisa Marie Dougherty suggests, "Never fall into the trap of getting on the bicycle every day with no set plan other than adding miles to your [training]." Dougherty also says to "plan out each week of training before doing a single workout." There are many ways that you can train for an ultra event, but there are some general elements that every training program should contain.

For additional information about training, and to create a training program just for you, get advice from a cycling coach or more experienced rider who is familiar with your fitness level and athletic experience. It is also helpful to read cycling books and magazines.

Mental Training

Remember that the most important facet to training is mental preparation and attitude.

—Lisa Mary Dougherty, *UltraCycling* magazine

Though your body must be trained to physically endure your chosen challenge, your mind generates the desire to reach your

Ultra training should include a variety of different terrains.

goal. It's important to have confidence and a positive attitude. To build confidence, it is helpful to visualize, or see yourself in your mind, achieving your goals. Visualization is a common practice among athletes. It helps them mentally prepare for the physical challenges ahead.

Another good mental exercise is to reverse negative thoughts. Negative thoughts, like "I can't climb well," are never helpful. It is important to replace them with positive thoughts, like "I am going to climb that hill steadily and smoothly."

Training Guidelines

Effort—Some days you should ride hard. Some days you should ride easy. During other rides you should pedal at a moderate pace, and some days you shouldn't ride at all. To complete your challenge, you need to push your body in training. But you also need to give it time to recover. When planning a week of training, mix up hard and easy days and be sure to throw in one or two days off the bike.

Terrain—The ride you are training for will likely have hills as well as flat sections. You should cover the same types of terrain in your training. Some days ride in the hills, other days ride on the flats, and some days do both.

Distance—Just like you mix up the intensity of your rides from day to day, you should also alter the length of your rides. While you should certainly ride long distances, it is important to ride short distances, too. Most programs suggest riding at least one longer ride per week. As avid cyclist and freelance writer Monique Cole notes on Explore.com, "One or two long rides per week are better training than several shorter rides."

Gradually Increase Training—Training programs should get harder each week. Start off riding fewer and easier miles, then increase the length and intensity of the rides each week until it's almost the day of the race. Be sure, however, to give yourself a week of easy, restful riding before the event. You want to be fresh for the big day.

Flexibility—Though it is important to have a training program and stick to it, it is also important to allow yourself to alter the program if it is not working. If you feel very tired and unmotivated to ride, take a rest day. If you're out on a ride and feeling great, put in a few extra miles. Feel free to alter your program in the way that works best for you.

Equipment

The most basic equipment you need in order to participate in a long-distance ride is a helmet, a bike, and a good attitude. It is very important to make sure that your bike is running smoothly, you have a helmet that fits you well and is comfortable, and you are excited and confident about the ride.

Moving Ahead

Once you have completed your first ultra challenge, you may find that you are ready to continue challenging yourself to ride in

Training gives ultra cyclists the best advantage for finishing races.

longer events or on more challenging courses. Joining a local cycling club is a great way to become more involved in the sport. Most clubs hold regular training rides, offer advice to new riders, put on events, and provide support for those interested in learning more about cycling.

Many cyclists have found that, by joining a club, they've gained access to other cyclists and information they wouldn't have found otherwise. There are cycling clubs located throughout the United States and Canada. To find one in your area, contact a local bike shop or search the Internet. Check the Ultra Info section in the back of this book to learn more.

Ultra cyclists need to be aware of a number of safety and health concerns. Riders must have proper safety gear, like a helmet, lights, and reflective tape and clothing. And because ultra riders spend a lot of time riding alone, they should be able to repair their bikes so that they do not wind up stranded far from home.

Ultra cycling tests the body's limits. The demands of the sport can lead to injury or ongoing physical problems. Ultra cyclists must

not only be aware of these potential problems but also know how to avoid them.

Safety on the Road

Riding on the open road can be peaceful and beautiful. But there is also automobile traffic that can endanger cyclists, especially those without proper safety equipment. And bicycles sometimes break. For the ill-equipped or unprepared cyclist, this means being stuck with no way to get home. In order to avoid these dangers, a cyclist should have the right gear, know how to repair his or her bicycle, strictly abide by the rules of the road, and be aware of traffic at all times.

A helmet should fit snugly and comfortably to properly protect the cyclist should he or she fall.

Helmets

The most important piece of safety gear for a cyclist is the helmet. It is an absolute must for any rider. A helmet can mean the difference between an annoying fall and a permanently damaging (or fatal) accident. Helmets come in many shapes, sizes, and colors. Different brands, models, and

It is wise to wear bright clothing and use reflector gear so that drivers are able to see you better.

sizes will fit each person differently. It is important to find one that fits snugly and comfortably.

Most helmets are approved by two organizations: the American National Standards Institute (ANSI) and the Snell Memorial Foundation (often referred to as Snell). Any ANSI/Snell-approved helmet has passed a number of tests that indicate it is safe to use. All cycling events require a cyclist to wear an ANSI/Snell-approved helmet.

Lights and Reflective Gear

Any cyclist planning to be out after dark must also have lights and reflective gear. Day or night, it is a good idea for a cyclist to wear brightly colored clothing during a ride. Front lights, which are white, allow the rider to see the road and be seen by drivers. Riders can choose from helmet-mounted lights or ones that mount on the handlebar. They can choose lights that use regular batteries or light systems that come with rechargeable batteries. Battery-operated lights are cheaper and weigh less, but they don't last as long. Light systems are brighter and last longer, but they are heavier and more expensive.

Rear lights, reflective gear, and bright clothing help make a cyclist even more visible to drivers. Reflective gear can come in the form of tape, which can be applied to the helmet and any part of the bike. There is also a lot of clothing made out of reflective fabric or with reflective material added to it. Rear lights, which are red, are small and can attach to the bike just below the seat (on the seat post) or to the back of the helmet. They generally come with the option to blink or remain a steady beam. Lights and reflective gear are required for all nighttime ultra events.

Learn to Fix Mechanical Problems

At some point, every cyclist experiences mechanical problems. As Lon Haldeman stated in an essay for *UltraCycling* magazine, "After working as a . . . mechanic for fifteen years on some very nice bikes, I realized that all bikes break." In that same essay, Haldeman offered some good advice regarding mechanical skills every rider should develop: "Every ultra rider should be able to: change and patch a tire and tube, install new brake or shift cables, change a spoke and true a wheel [make a wheel straight], repair a broken chain, [and] realize and fix a problem before [getting] stranded."

An ultra cyclist changes a flat tire as competitors pass her during a professional mountain-bike race.

In order to learn how to perform these tasks, you could purchase a bicycle repair book (see the Ultra Reading section at the end of this book for suggestions) or check with local bike shops to find one that offers maintenance and repair classes.

Along with learning to work on his or her bike, an ultra rider needs to carry the tools to do the job. There are many tools on the market, called multitools, that are made specifically to take along on a ride. They are lightweight and compact, which makes them convenient and easy to carry. Multitools can be found at most bike shops. A cyclist should also have all the tools needed to repair the most common mechanical problem: flat tires.

Bike Fit

It is very important for a cyclist to fit on his or her bike properly. Improper fit can lead to great discomfort and even injury. This is especially true for ultra cyclists because they spend so much time on the bike. Key points to consider when fitting a rider to a bike are frame size, handlebar width, and saddle position.

In general, the frame fits a rider if there is a one- or two-inch gap between the rider's crotch and the top tube when the rider is standing over the bike with no shoes on. (This information is specific to fitting a rider on a road bike. Proper mountain-bike fitting is slightly different.)

Another important measurement is the reach to the handlebars. Ideally, a rider's upper body should be at about a 45-degree angle to the top tube when the rider's hands are resting on the brake hoods and the elbows are relaxed. The next consideration is saddle height. The general rule of thumb is that, with the pedal down and the foot flatly resting on it, there should be a slight bend in the rider's

How your bike fits can make a difference in how you perform, and in how comfortable you are, in a marathon cycling event.

knee. A rider should also make sure that the handlebars are not too wide or narrow. Handlebars should be about the same width as the rider's shoulders.

These adjustments and measurements help ensure that the bike fits well and doesn't cause the rider pain or injury. But they are only basic guidelines. They do not work perfectly for every rider. It is important for cyclists to always be aware of pain or discomfort and adjust their bicycles as necessary. It is not uncommon for a rider to experience pain in the knees, lower back, upper back, neck, hands, or feet. But many of these problems can be fixed with minor adjustments to the bicycle. Many bike shops offer services to help riders set up their bikes properly. And many ultra riders spend years adjusting and correcting their position so that it is just right.

Eating and Drinking

When a cyclist rides for many hours, he or she needs to remain hydrated and well fed. It is very important for ultra cyclists to eat and drink continually during a long or intense ride. Otherwise, the cyclist could experience severe dehydration, which can cause stomach problems and even put the rider in the hospital. According to ultra cyclist Steve Born, in an article written for *UltraCycling* magazine, "It is now believed that about twenty-four ounces of fluids per hour is the most a body can absorb." Every ultra cyclist needs to continually consume this much liquid throughout a ride or event to avoid dehydration.

Too little food can result in "bonking"—a condition marked by extremely low energy and loss of motivation due to lack of fuel. To avoid bonking, riders must "train" their stomachs to consume

As in all ultra sports, it is important to remain hydrated.

enough food to keep them going. Born notes that "exercising at maximum intensity level and assimilating [consuming] a lot of calories hour after hour are not things that the body would normally prefer to do simultaneously."

Bonking and dehydration can be very serious problems, especially if they occur when a rider is alone on a long training ride.

A Final Word About Safety and Health

Ultra cycling is a demanding sport. A rider needs to be well prepared to remain safe and healthy. By abiding by these few simple precautions, he or she is sure to have a more enjoyable experience.

Ultra Gear

In the preceding chapter, we discussed some of the safety equipment you need to participate in ultra cycling, such as a helmet, lights, and reflective clothing. In this chapter, we will discuss some of the other basic equipment long-distance riders use. While cyclists may debate which equipment is best, they all agree on one thing: Comfort is the most important factor.

Bike

To ride, you will need a bike. There are three basic types of bicycles: mountain, road, and hybrid. Mountain bikes are used for riding on dirt. Hybrid bicycles are made for comfortable cruising on paved streets. Road bikes, the choice of ultra riders who ride on the road, are the most efficient bikes and are built for speed.

A road bike *(left)* and a hybrid bike *(right)*

Road bikes have narrow tires and are very lightweight. They have a handlebar called a "drop bar," which curves down. Road bikes also have a lot of gears—up to twenty-seven! Bike shops typically carry a variety of road bikes from several different manufacturers and of various levels of quality. With so many options, how do riders choose? In an essay written for *UltraCycling* magazine, cyclist Lon Haldeman summed up the bike-choosing process in a very basic and useful way: "I feel an ultra bike should be treated as a tool toward results. Lightweight, durability, comfort, and efficiency for you should be considered when shopping for your new bike. Buy the best bike for your budget. Then learn to use it, learn to fix it, and keep training."

Aerodynamics

One of the strongest forces a rider confronts on the road is wind. For this reason, riders try to make themselves able to easily cut through the wind; they work on being aerodynamic. This is one of the reasons many riders choose road bikes; they allow the rider to ride in the most aerodynamic position.

You may have seen the Tour de France on television or riders out on the road and noticed that they lean over their bikes, bringing their bodies as close to the bike as possible. If a rider sits upright (as one does on a mountain or hybrid bicycle), the wind pushes against his or her upper body. Riders lean over to stay out of the wind, to be aerodynamic. This technique saves a lot of energy and enables a cyclist to go faster using less effort.

The Contact Points

Contact points are those places where the rider and the bike meet, like the handlebars, pedals, and saddle or seat. Riders use equipment like gloves, shoes, and shorts to cushion this contact. Because this equipment is essential to riding comfort, you should

Mark Patton rests his forearms on his bike's aerobars as he rides with the Colorado sunset during the fourth day of the Race Across America on June 21, 2000.

carefully investigate and try out these pieces of equipment before heading out on a long ride.

Handlebars and Gloves

A common problem among cyclists is numb hands and wrist pain. These conditions result from leaning on the handlebars for hours on end. To help avoid numbness and pain, riders cushion the handlebars with padded tape. They also wear cycling gloves. These gloves are padded as well, providing additional cushioning between the hands and bars.

Most ultra cyclists also use aerobars. Aerobars are handlebars that attach to the regular drop bars. They allow a rider to lean over the bike to be more aerodynamic. Also, as riders lean their elbows and forearms on the aerobars, no pressure is put upon the hands and wrists.

Saddles, Saddle Covers, and Shorts

One of the most common complaints that cyclists (especially new cyclists) have is a sore rear end. But there is really no need to suffer. There are many different types of saddles to choose from: ones with a hole in the middle, ones with gel padding, gender-specific models, and more. Cyclists should experiment with many types of saddles in order to find one that fits them well.

Some riders also like to use a saddle cover. These are pads that fit over the saddle and add extra padding. After hundreds of miles, even the most comfortable saddle may start to feel a little hard. It never hurts to have a saddle cover, just in case.

Cycling shorts are another must for the ultra cyclist. Bike shorts are padded to cushion the body where it meets the saddle, and they are made out of material that "wicks," or pulls moisture such as sweat, away from the body and then dries very quickly.

As any rider who has experienced saddle discomfort can tell you, a good shorts and saddle combination can mean the difference between a pleasant ride and complete misery.

Shoes and Pedals

Riders use shoes made specifically for cycling. They fit snugly and have a hard sole that does not bend. They also have cleats that clip into the pedals. Anyone who has skied will be familiar with boots that clip into the skis. Cycling shoes and pedals work the same way. When clipped in, the rider's shoe and pedal become one unit. To unclip, the rider only has to turn his heel outward, and the shoe is freed from the pedal.

This shoe/pedal combination makes the cyclist very efficient—the rider basically becomes a part of the bike. Unfortunately, the hardness of the sole and tightness of the shoe can cause foot numbness and pain. A rider needs to choose shoes that fit well but that are also comfortable, pay attention to any foot pain, and make adjustments if numbness and pain arise.

Clip pedals help riders' shoes from slipping off and keep riders from losing momentum.

Monitoring Equipment

Though not absolutely necessary, there are two items that many cyclists use to monitor their progress and their bodies: the cyclometer and the heart rate monitor.

Cyclometer

Riders often use cycling computers called cyclometers to monitor their riding. Most cyclometers, which mount on top of the handlebars, show the rider's speed, distance traveled, time of day, and average speed.

Heart Rate Monitor

A heart rate monitor allows a rider to see his or her heart rate, which indicates how hard the body is working. This tool helps the rider monitor how his or her body is reacting to the harsh demands of an ultra ride.

More to Consider

In this chapter, we covered some of the basic equipment that long-distance cyclists use. There is more equipment available and, additionally, more technical information that serious racers and experienced cyclists consider when making equipment choices. Generally, as a cyclist becomes more involved in the sport, he or she will collect the information and experience necessary to make the best equipment decisions. In fact, those who are very competitive consider every detail of each piece of equipment; they leave nothing to chance.

5 Ultra Tips

Experience is an important factor in ultra racing. Knowing ahead of time what to expect and how to deal with the unusual, painful, and sometimes scary situations that commonly occur during an ultra race can mean the difference between a successful ride and unnecessary suffering.

Common Reactions to Ultra Stress

Ultra races push the mind and body to the limit. Pushed this far, they can react in strange and occasionally scary ways. For riders who know in advance what to expect, these experiences can be easier and less frightening to deal with.

Emotions

It is not uncommon for a rider to become very emotional or depressed during an ultra ride. The physical and mental strain combined with extreme fatigue and lack of sleep can push anyone to the

breaking point. Ultra cyclist Jeff "Jaguar" Martin describes one such instance during his 2000 Furnace Creek 508 ride.

> *At slightly past 5:00 AM we arrive at the top of Salsberry Pass . . . For the first time in the race I am really starting to "feel the pain." Nothing specific, just pure exhaustion . . . So we're all there at the top of Salsberry Pass. One second I'm joking with the crew and in a split second after that, my emotions have caught up to me, and I'm sobbing uncontrollably.*

Reactions such as depression and emotional exhaustion can be overwhelming and can cause self-doubt to plague a rider's mind. It is important for a rider to realize that these feelings are happening because the body and mind are being pushed to their limits and that the emotions are temporary. As a cyclist continues to ride, the feelings should pass.

Hallucinations

> *It's the middle of the day. You have been riding almost nonstop for hundreds of miles on your way to completing the single longest bicycle race in the world: the Race Across America. Then you decide to stop. You tell your crew that you have to wait for your friends. A little confused, they quickly realize that you are hallucinating. Fatigue is taking its toll on your mind. Seeing that you are not in danger, they tell you to get back on your bike, your friends will catch up. You decide this is a good idea and dutifully remount your bike and begin to ride.*

Marathon cyclists often go through a wide range of emotions during a race.

Sound unbelievable? It's true. Ultra cycling pioneer Susan Notorangelo experienced this hallucination during one of her several RAAM races. Ultra racer Muffy Ritz says, "The most frightening times I've had in ultra races (such as RAAM) are when I am hallucinating. It's a scary feeling." She continues, "I've hallucinated such things as 100-foot farmers, cowboys, lawn ornaments that went on for hours, dead dachshunds, thousands of white shoes, and flea markets."

Though they may sound strange and, for some, be frightening, hallucinations are fairly common during multiday cycling events. RAAM racer Mark Patton has come to accept them as a part of racing. Unlike Ritz, he speaks with some fondness about the many hallucinations he has had. During one RAAM race, he continually saw the cartoon characters Ren and Stimpy; during another, he watched the road turn into patterns that looked like tattoos.

Though strange, hallucinations are usually nothing to worry about. According to many experienced cyclists, they are simply the result of poor nutrition, something that novice riders tend to experience. And Notorangelo noted that as long as the rider is aware that he or she is riding a bike, it's all right to continue riding.

Sometimes the Body Says No

It is not uncommon for the body to stop absorbing food and water when a rider is participating in an ultra event.

> At around 8:30 AM (after twenty-seven and a half hours of riding) my stomach shuts down. I was just riding along . . . when I realized that my stomach was very bloated and starting to ache slightly. Not too much pain but definitely not good. Mostly I was annoyed . . . The next thing I know, there's Steve [an experienced racer and friend] standing alongside the road out in the middle of nowhere . . . First off, Steve says don't worry, it's quite normal. He says . . . "Welcome to the world of ultra cycling!"

This was another of Jeff Martin's 2000 FC508 experiences. Though very unpleasant—and generally, like hallucinations, the result of poor nutrition—it is no reason to quit. But it also cannot be ignored. Consuming something to settle the stomach, taking a short break, and going to the bathroom can help a rider get the

Many organized ultra rides have rest stops where riders can refuel.

digestive system working properly again. This is just what Martin did, and within a short period of time he was feeling fine.

Pacing

In order to go the distance, a racer must ride a steady pace. He or she doesn't want to push the body too hard (or not hard enough) at any point in the race. A common problem many riders experience is riding too fast in the beginning and then not having enough energy left to finish. According to Mike "Whale" Wilson, a rider who has finished the FC508 several times, "Pacing will be the most important aspect of the race."

One tool that many riders use to monitor their pace is a heart rate monitor. This way a rider can make sure that his or her effort is consistent throughout the race.

Plan for the Unexpected

It is very important for an ultra racer to go into the race with a solid plan of action. The rider should plan how much sleep he or she will get, how fast he or she expects to ride over each part of the course—every detail of the race should be considered. However, it is also important to be prepared for the unplanned. The rider and crew have to be open to unexpected changes, learn to put aside frustration and anxiety over not sticking strictly to the schedule, and simply move ahead by factoring in each situation that presents itself.

Bring More of Everything

One way to be prepared for the unplanned is to bring more equipment and clothing than supposedly necessary. A rider never knows when or how severely the weather might change. And bikes break. A support crew should have tools and extra parts for the bicycle. As John Stamstad, one of the most experienced ultra distance riders, advises, "Have a spare for everything."

The Mental Game

Ultra riders face numerous mental changes—fatigue, frustration, hallucinations, depression, loneliness. And in the face of all of

Marathon cycling can be a lonely sport—sometimes even at the finish line when you are far behind the pack.

these, they must always be determined to finish. To stay motivated, riders can practice many tricks while they train and use them during races to help them keep going.

Break It Down

Thinking about an entire race at the beginning can be overwhelming. It is helpful, even critical, to mentally break the race into sections. This is a trick Lon Haldeman has used often. During their successful bid to set the tandem transcontinental record (with a time of seven days and fourteen hours), Haldeman and tandem partner Pete Penseyres broke the course down into ten-mile sections. They never thought about more than the next ten miles. Haldeman says he "lost track of the race" until he was at the finish. Similarly, when riding his double transcontinental ride (from New York City to Los Angeles and back), he focused on thinking only of riding from one town to the next.

Goals

Setting clear and specific goals will enable a rider to stay focused and motivated, even in the toughest of times. Riders can set some goals before the race, such as, "I want to reach 300 miles before I take a break." Other goals will develop during the race, like, "I'm going to get over that mountain range before sunset." Susan Notorangelo used this latter goal-setting plan to push herself through one of her most intense ultra experiences and win the 1985 RAAM. Two hundred miles from the finish, she moved into first place. Low on energy, but determined to win the race, Notorangelo put her head down, hammered to the finish line, and crossed it first. A realistic and challenging goal can be just the motivation a rider needs to keep going strong to the end.

The Lonely Road

Riding in an ultra race can be very lonely. A rider is out on the bike for hours and hours. To combat loneliness, many riders use two-way radios so that they can talk to their crew. This also helps keep the crew in touch with how the rider is feeling.

A sound system mounted on the outside of the follow vehicle—so that the music can be heard by the rider—can also help. Most riders

The lonely road

use this and have the crew play motivational music that inspires and entertains. It's a great way to keep the mind from thinking about the miles ahead.

A Final Word

Experience and the advice of others are very helpful to all ultra racers. Many riders find that working closely with a veteran of the sport greatly improves their performance. There is always more to learn. Every ultra race is a new adventure and a new challenge, which is what drives so many riders to keep coming back for more.

In the ultra world, there are several ways that a rider can test his or her abilities. These challenges can be broken down into two categories: races and rides. Many in the ultra world, such as those in the randonneuring community, wish to test themselves by completing long distances in a certain amount of time. They prefer long-distance organized rides. These are timed events in which no winner is announced. And though these rides are not competitions, riders often use these events to push themselves to complete the distance as fast as they can.

For others, the ultimate test is racing. Racing provides a competitive atmosphere and puts the rider in a position to push his or her limits as far as possible against others who are doing the same.

Why Ultra?

Before discussing ultra competition, it is important to answer an often-asked question: Why? Why would anyone want to push his or her body to such a degree? Many ultra cyclists do it for the adventure. For others, especially those who enter the sport before they have access to a car, riding represents freedom and independence. Many relish the challenge and fitness gained from training and racing. Chris Kostman speaks of the confidence he has gained from participating in the sport, which has inspired him to pursue other interests with equal vigor. There is also the joy of making friends in the supportive and welcoming ultra community: There are numerous stories about how helpful and friendly the ultra cycling community is to both newcomers and veterans. Ultra cycling provides a place where you can have an extraordinary, life-altering experience. It provides an opportunity to stretch the limits of possibility.

Races

There are many ultra distance races. Two of most prestigious road races are the Race Across America (RAAM) and the Furnace Creek 508 (FC508). For those who prefer mountain biking, two standouts—Montezuma's Revenge and the Leadville 100—provide supreme challenges.

Race Across America (RAAM)

Since 1982 the Race Across America has brought together the best endurance cyclists to compete in the world's toughest race. Racing in RAAM is more than a cycling event. The physical extremes will test the limits of any rider.

The logistics and planning will challenge the sanity of any support team. The emotional highs and lows will be remembered by everyone involved with the race.

—Lon Haldeman, RAAM Web site

RAAM is certainly the most prestigious of all ultra cycling events. Riders come from all around the world to participate in this great challenge. It is undoubtedly the longest and toughest nonstop cycling race. The distance may vary slightly each year, as the course usually changes. However, it is never fewer than 2,900 miles and has not yet been longer than 3,200 miles. The winner usually completes the course in just over eight to ten days, depending on the length of the route and the conditions the rider experiences. In order to do this, a rider does not sleep more than a couple of hours each day, if that!

During RAAM, the racer is supported by a group of people—the crew—who follow in vehicles, usually vans or motor

Sean Hogan's crew follows him for support during the Race Across America on July 30, 1995.

homes. The crew helps motivate the rider, makes sure he or she has food and water, and keeps him or her on the race course—basically, the crew does everything they can to allow the racer to focus completely on riding as fast as he or she can.

Depending on the course, a rider might pass over several mountain ranges or through the desert, or suffer through endless miles of boring, flat landscape. A racer may experience weather that is rainy, freezing cold, windy, or humid and hot. These factors, combined with all the other unknown variables (you never know when a follow vehicle is going to break down or if the racer is going to have terrible stomach problems, blisters, or neck pain) and the distance, make this race extremely challenging. It is the ultimate test.

Furnace Creek 508 (FC508)

The FC508 is, according to its Web site, "the premier 500-mile race in the world." The "original and longest running" RAAM-qualifying race (riders wanting to do RAAM must qualify by completing other races within a certain time limit) was started in 1983. Since 1989, this 508-mile race has run through the California desert, covering ten major climbs along the way. As during RAAM, riders are supported by crews. Racers have forty-eight hours to complete the course, though most finish long before this deadline.

Montezuma's Revenge

Promoted as the "World's Worst Race," Montezuma's Revenge is known as the toughest ultra mountain-bike race. This twenty-four-hour challenge takes place in the Colorado Rocky Mountains. The course is all at a very high altitude, which, among other things, leaves people

A racer falls in the snow. Be extra careful when riding in the snow.

short of breath (there is less oxygen at high altitudes), can cause digestive problems, and promotes dehydration. The weather in this area can vary from cold and snowing to hot and dry. And the course is not marked! Some of it does not even have a trail to follow, and riders must "bushwhack" through and create their own path! To date, no one has completed the entire course within the twenty-four-hour time limit.

Leadville 100

Like Montezuma's Revenge, the Leadville 100 pits racers against the difficult terrain, high altitude, and inclement weather of

Colorado's Rocky Mountains. Though extremely tough, this race has no shortage of participants. In fact, the promoters get so many entry forms they now use a lottery system to decide who will participate. Each year, just over 700 lucky riders get their chance to complete the 100 grueling miles. For their intense effort, riders are awarded prizes that vary based on their finishing times. Riders who finish within thirteen hours receive a medal; those coming in under twelve get a silver belt buckle; and those who finish in under nine hours win the prestigious La Plata Grande, or Big Buckle, made of silver and gold.

Rides

For those wishing to complete challenging distances without the pressure of racing—to improve their level of ultra fitness, qualify for more challenging events, or just to test their limits—there are many rides throughout North America in which they can participate. In addition to the numerous standard-distance brevets promoted in the randonneuring community, there are centuries, double centuries, and more. The UMCA (on the Web at www.ultracycling.com) and Randonneurs USA (www.rusa.org) both provide helpful information about upcoming events.

At the End of the Day

Ultra distance racing and riding provide people with an opportunity to test their mental and physical limits. "You're reduced to a basic level," says rider Kevin Griffin. "You're not even who you were when you started." The difficulty and intensity of riding

Ultra racing takes you places both beautiful and challenging.

long miles brings out undiscovered personal strengths and weaknesses. It is also enjoyable and exciting, a way for someone to explore unknown terrain. For anyone with the interest and a bike (and a helmet), the challenge and adventure are out there waiting to be discovered.

Glossary

aerobars Handlebars that attach to drop bars and allow riders to get into very leaned-over or aerodynamic positions.

aerodynamic Cuts through wind well.

arm warmers Garments worn by cyclists that cover the arm between the bottom of the sleeve and the wrist. They look like sleeves but have elastic at the non-wrist end.

bonk To run out of energy and motivation because of a lack of fuel.

booties Garments that cover cycling shoes. Used in cold weather.

bottom bracket The part of the bicycle that connects the crankarms to the bicycle frame.

brevet A name for a long-distance (randonneuring) bicycle event.

century As a cycling term, a 100-mile ride.

crankarm The part of the bicycle that attaches the pedal to the bicycle frame.

double century As a cycling term, a 200-mile ride.

down tube The part of the bicycle frame that runs from the head tube to where the crankarms meet the bike (called the bottom bracket).

drafting Riding behind another cyclist to avoid being in the wind.

drop bars The type of handlebars found on a road bike.

efficient Able to do something with the least amount of effort.

fork The part of the bicycle frame that runs between the handlebars and the front wheel.

hallucinate To see or hear something that is not really there.

head tube   The part of the bicycle frame that goes between the handlebars and the fork.

hybrid bicycle   A bicycle made for comfortable cruising; so called because it is a cross between a mountain bike and road bike.

interval   As a training term, refers to riding hard over a short, specific period of time. An interval usually lasts between thirty seconds and five minutes. Intervals help train the body to ride faster.

leg warmers   Garments worn by cyclists that cover the portion of the leg between the bottom of the shorts and the ankle. Leg warmers look like pant legs but have elastic at the non-ankle end.

mountain bike   A bicycle made to be ridden on dirt.

randonnée   A randonneuring event; also called a brevet.

randonneuring   A long-distance bicycle event, the rules for which were created over 100 years ago.

road bike   A bicycle made to be ridden efficiently on paved roads.

seat tube   The part of the bicycle frame that runs from the saddle to where the crankarms meet the bike.

stem   The bicycle part that attaches the handlebars to the bike.

time trial   A type of cycling race in which the rider is timed over a specific course. The rider who completes the course in the least amount of time wins.

top tube   The part of the bicycle frame that runs from where the seat joins the bike to where the handlebars join the bike.

wick   As a cycling clothing term, to pull moisture away from the skin.

FC508
AdventureCORPS
11718 Barrington Court, #342
Los Angeles, CA 90049-2930

Furnace Creek 508
Chris Kostman, race director
AdventureCORPS
549 Vistamount Court
Berkeley, CA 94708-1243
(510) 528-3263
e-mail: chris@adventurecorps.com
Web site: http://www.the508.com

Leadville 100
P.O. Box 487
Leadville, CO 80461
(719) 486-3502
Web site: http://www.leadvilletrail100.com/LT100bik.html

RAAM and PAC Tour
P.O. Box 303
202 Prairie Pedal Lane
Sharon, WI 53585
(262) 736-BIKE (2453)
Web site: http://www.pactour.com

Randonneurs USA
10 Bliss Mine Road
Middletown, RI 02842
(401) 847-1715
Web site: http://www.rusa.org

24 Hours of Adrenalin
7321 Victoria Park Avenue, Suite #8
Markham, ON L3R 2Z8
(905) 944-9436
Fax: (905) 944-9434
Web site: http://www.24hoursofadrenalin.com

Ultra Marathon Cycling Association (UMCA)
P.O. Box 18028
Boulder, CO 80308-1028
(303) 545-9566
e-mail: UMCAHQ@aol.com
Web site: http://www.ultracycling.com

Baker, Arnie. *Bicycling Medicine: Cycling Nutrition, Physiology, and Injury Prevention and Treatment for Riders of All Levels.* New York: Fireside, 1998.

Baker, Arnie. *Smart Cycling: Successful Training and Racing for Riders of All Levels.* New York: Simon & Schuster, 1997.

Ballantine, Richard. *Richard's Bicycle Repair Manual.* New York: Dorling Kindersley Publishing, Inc., 1994.

Bicycling Magazine editors. *Bicycling Magazine's Long-Distance Cycling.* Emmaus, PA: Rodale Press, 1993.

Burke, Edmund R. *Serious Cycling.* 2nd ed. Champaign, IL: Human Kinetics Publishers, 2002.

Burke, Edmund, R., and Ed Pavelka. *The Complete Book of Long-Distance Cycling: Build the Strength, Skills and Confidence to Ride as Far as You Want.* Emmaus, PA: Rodale Press, 2000.

Doyle, Ken, and Eric Schmitz. *Weight Training for Cyclists.* Boulder, CO: VeloPress, 1998.

Friel, Joe. *The Cyclist's Training Bible: A Complete Training Guide for the Competitive Road Cyclist.* Boulder, CO: VeloPress, 1997.

Friel, Joe. *The Mountain Biker's Training Bible: A Complete Training Guide for the Competitive Mountain Biker.* Boulder, CO: VeloPress, 2000.

Kita, Joe, ed. *Bicycling Magazine's Training for Fitness and Endurance.* Emmaus, PA: Rodale Press, 1990.

Miller, Saul, and Peggy Maass Hill. *Sports Psychology for Cyclists.* Boulder, CO: VeloPress, 1999.

Steamaker, Rob. *Serious Training for Endurance Athletes.* 2nd ed. Champaign, IL: Human Kinetics Publishers, 1996.

Van der Plas, Rob. *Bicycle Repair Step by Step: The Full-Color Manual of Bicycle Maintenance and Repair.* San Francisco: Bicycle Books, 1994.

Index

Credits

Acknowledgments

My deepest thanks go out to those amazing athletes who shared their ultra experiences and expertise: Lon Haldeman, Susan Notorangelo, Mark Patton, Rod and Brenda Kish, Muffy Ritz, and Chris Kostman. Thank you to Chad Grenier and Jennifer Wise for their promptness in answering my questions and their breadth of knowledge. Thank you to Bill Bryant for his historical knowledge and willingness to share it. And, as always, thank you to Kerry Callahan, who helps me get words on paper.

About the Author

Chérie Turner is a writer, editor, and cyclist. She lives in San Anselmo, California.

Photo Credits

Cover, pp. 4,6, 27 © AP/Wide World Photos; © pp. 5, 48 © Pascal Rondeau/Corbis; pp. 8, 10, 12 © Hulton/Getty; pp.15, 50 © Jim Gensheimer/Corbis; pp. 32 (hybrid bike), 19 (flat terrain), 28 © Karl Weatherly/Corbis; p. 19 (hill) © Julie Habel/Corbis; p. 22 © Tom Putt/STL/Icon SMI; p. 23 © Paul J. Sutton/Corbis; p. 24 © Dave Teel/Corbis; p. 25 © Lee Cohen/Corbis; p. 30 © Ken Redding/Corbis; p. 31 © Robert Trubia/Corbis; p. 32 (street bike) © Rick Doyle/Corbis; p. 34, 46 © Brian Bahr/Allsport; p. 36 © Yann Guichaoua/Agency Vandystadt/Allsport; p. 38 © Don Hammond/Corbis; p. 40 © Corbis; p. 42 © Tom Bean/Corbis; p. 44 © Ales Fevzer/Corbis; p. 52 © Duomo/Corbis; p. 54 © Randy Lincks/Corbis.

Design and Layout

Thomas Forget